IMAGES
of England

MOSELEY
BALSALL HEATH
AND HIGHGATE

IMAGES
of England

MOSELEY
BALSALL HEATH
AND HIGHGATE

Compiled by

Marian Baxter and Peter Drake

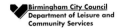
Birmingham City Council
Department of Leisure and
Community Services

TEMPUS

First published 1996, reprinted 2002
Copyright © Marian Baxter and Peter Drake, 1996

Tempus Publishing Limited
The Mill, Brimscombe Port,
Stroud, Gloucestershire, GL5 2QG

ISBN 0 7524 0680 9

Typesetting and origination by
Tempus Publishing Limited
Printed in Great Britain by
Midway Colour Print, Wiltshire

Contents

Acknowledgements

Our thanks go to Birmingham City Council, Department of Leisure and Community Services, Libraries and Learning, for allowing us to use their photographs.

Thanks to Martin Flynn, Central Library Manager, Birmingham Central Library, who did the negotiations with the publisher and encouraged us to put this volume together.

Special thanks to Geoff Cashmore who sorted out the computer every time Marian Baxter pressed the wrong button.

Thanks to the staff of the Birmingham Local Studies and History Department and the families of the two authors for their patience.

Introduction

Choosing these photographs from the collections in the Local Studies and History section of Birmingham Central Library was both challenging and rewarding. The challenge was to select from the sheer numbers of previously unpublished photographs - there are several boxes of photographs of Highbury Hall for example - while many photographs taken of Highgate before redevelopment in the 1960s by Birmingham's Public Works Department only exist as glass negatives. The reward was to contribute to the history of three fascinating and differing districts. The contrasts between the areas are more vivid because of the small geographic area covered. From the inner city squalor of late nineteenth century courtyards in Highgate to the splendours of Moseley Hall and Park may be less than a couple of miles, but they reflect different worlds and different communities. The link is the Alcester Turnpike, now the Highgate Middleway and the Moseley Road linking the city centre with Moseley, Balsall Heath and Highgate and providing many of the photographs reproduced here.

The geographic location, due south of Birmingham city centre, was crucial to the growth of this whole area in the late eighteenth century and through the Victorian age. It meant that manufacturers, traders and other prosperous employers, with premises close to the centre of Birmingham, looked to the area to build their homes safe in the knowledge that the prevailing winds would not send industrial smoke over their newly built houses. However only isolated houses in Highgate and Balsall Heath, particularly those in Highgate Square, still provide a reminder of that bygone time. Much of Moseley, though, is a testimony to the fruits, for some, of Victorian prosperity. The River Rea running along the western border of the district also contributed to the area's development. Farms survived into the last century in the meadows of Balsall Heath alongside a clear river, while families strolled out on Sundays into the almost rural splendour of the district. Balsall Heath, prior to the main phase of house building in the mid Victorian period, was Birmingham's second most desirable suburb, behind only Edgbaston, its neighbour across the River Rea. The lack of a canal in the area limited the industrial development and partly explains the absence of substantial factories.

From the late nineteenth century the history of Balsall Heath and Highgate is bound up with the role of Birmingham Corporation, or the City Council as it has now become. From the first publicly owned park in the city, Highgate Park opened in 1871, through to the splendid facilities of Balsall Heath Library and Swimming Baths and numerous schools, the City has actively tried to meet the needs and aspirations of a densely populated area. Housing has been the catalyst for change in the district, most graphically illustrated in the photographs of the

Emily Street area of Highgate. There you have a microcosm of twentieth century housing development starting with the mixed courtyards and back-to-back dwellings inherited from the Victorians, through to inter-war tenement-style blocks, to the more mixed housing standing today. Other factors for change have been the effects of German bombing, the recent building of the Middle Ring Road in the form of the Highgate and Belgrave Middleways, the changing industrial character of the area and the diverse ethnic composition of Balsall Heath in particular. Communities have been broken up and re-formed. The history of local cinemas reflects some of these changes. A number of Birmingham's earliest cinemas, several along the Moseley Road, provide a real community focus. Their heyday was in the 1920s and 1930s but after the Second World War they started to fall on hard times and to close. They re-opened as Asian cinemas and enjoyed a fairly transitory popularity before closing again in the early eighties and most have now been demolished. It is only in recent years that Balsall Heath, through its vibrantly mixed population, has rediscovered its community spirit. The Central Mosque on the Belgrave Middleway is just one of the many physical manifestations of that new confidence.

Whereas very little of Balsall Heath and Highgate is still recognizable from early photographs it is a very different picture with Moseley. The photographs of Moseley Village and St Mary's Row at the heart of the suburb, taken before the turn of the century, show scenes very little changed today except in the much heavier traffic. Likewise most of the lavish houses built last century in the Wake Green area survive. Moseley has its own character with over twenty-five listed buildings, a private park created from the Moseley Hall estate, the Chamberlains' family home, Highbury, and even the Moseley Bog. It is still the 'pleasant suburb' described in *Kelly's Directory* in 1896. In the late nineteenth century the building of exclusive houses in the Park Hill Area was designed to create a buffer between the rapidly expanding Balsall Heath and the tranquil and more rural Moseley. Even transport played its part in accentuating the differences. The refusal to put workmen's trains on the Birmingham to Gloucester line and the absence of third class tickets on the trams helped to maintain Moseley's exclusivity.

Even in its arts and sports facilities Moseley has a middle class feel to it. Rugby, golf and cricket clubs have flourished while Moseley has strong literary connections, most notably in J.R.R. Tolkein's depiction of scenes from his boyhood in Moseley in his fantasies. Moseley's music connections stretch from the well known Harrison subscription concerts organised by Percy Harrison of Moseley from 1870 to 1917, to today's success of the Moseley based group Ocean Colour Scene with their best selling CD *Moseley Shoals*. The proximity of Birmingham University has given a decidedly student and cosmopolitan flavour to the streets and pubs of Moseley.

All three suburbs have had to face major challenges. Highgate has seen the destruction of its inner city community spirit as well as the sub-standard housing, to be replaced by an uneasy mixture of industrial and residential development. Balsall Heath and north Moseley have endured a red-light image since the last part of the nineteenth century, while, in the late 1960s and 1970s, Moseley residents faced a severe problem with vagrancy. Immigration has brought new and exciting challenges and transformed the character of some parts of the area. Despite these problems, succeeding generations have taken forward the spirit of community and self-improvement which features prominently in these photographs, and have created suburbs which have both interesting and invigorating histories but which have also retained a proud community spirit.

One

Houses

Old Cottage, Edgbaston Lane, Balsall Heath, 1892.

Old Cottage, Edgbaston Lane. Edgbaston Lane became Edgbaston Road in the 1870s and is still the main road from Moseley to the Balsall Heath Road.

Opposite: The home of the Tolkiens from 1896 to 1900 was at No. 5 Gracewell (now No. 264 Wake Green Road). See page 36 for a description of J.R.R. Tolkein's time in Moseley.

Salisbury Road, No. 59. Built in 1897 this substantial Arts and Crafts house was designed by Joseph Crouch and Edmund Butler. The house is raised in a banked garden on the corner of Salisbury and Amesbury Road. It has two storeys and an attic, of assymetrical design, is of red brick with an off centre three storey entrance tower. The house shows an effective combination of materials and varied emphasis to each elevation. In 1910 it was occupied by Mr F.T. Machin who lived there for nearly thirty years. It was bought by Mr N.P. Piller around the time of the Second World War and sold to the Birmingham Diocesan Board of of Finance in 1967. It returned to private ownership in 1985.

Old house, now demolished, on the Alcester Road, Moseley, opposite Park Hill, *c.* 1900.

Amesbury Court, Amesbury Road, Moseley. Amesbury Road was one of the last residential roads to be carved out of the Taylor Estate. With the exception of No. 41 and some of the more recent buildings, the houses were built on one side of the road only. The houses from No. 4 to No. 38 were all built between 1906 and 1911 when the district became part of Birmingham. Amesbury Court was designed by W.H. Bidlake.

The Dingle, Wake Green Road, Moseley.

Pitmaston, Moor Green Lane, viewed from the tennis lawn.

Houses on Moseley Road, 1948.

The premises of H. and R. Scott at No. 163 Moseley Road and No. 157, Andrews' Components, press works, photographed in 1948.

Houses on Sherlock Street and St Lukes Road prior to demolition for redevelopment, 1968.

Houses in No. 9 Court, Adelaide Street, Highgate, c. 1905.

A view of No. 26 Court, Gooch Street, *c.* 1905.

Unnumbered houses in Highgate Square, Moseley Road, *c.* 1905. This view shows the high class dwellings built in the early nineteenth century when Highgate Square became the focal point of development in the area.

Highgate Square, Moseley Road, *c.* 1905.

Number 3 Court, Darwin Street, Highgate before reconstruction, *c.* 1905.

Number 3 Court, Darwin Street, *c.* 1905.

Houses at the back of No. 82 Dymoke Street after reconstruction, *c*. 1905.

Numbers 5 and 6 at the back of No. 61 Clement Street after repairs, *c*. 1905.

Flats under construction in Gooch Street as part of the post war redevelopment schemes, 1952.

Gooch Street flats under construction.

Emily Street, 1934. This view of Emily Street junction with Dymoke Street in Highgate shows the juxtaposition of houses, pubs and small shops which characterised much of Birmingham's inner city housing. The Council planned to build 7,000 new dwellings as part of a major slum clearance scheme. A five acre site centred on Emily Street and bounded by Angelina, Dymoke, Leopold and Vaughton Streets, was chosen as the site of a major new housing development.

Emily Street, 1937. It was originally planned to build maisonettes on the site but surprisingly, at a time of high employment, a shortage of skilled labourers, especially plasterers and bricklayers, meant that the Council looked at alternative schemes. Based on contemporary Eastern European housing it was decided to hold an architectural competition to provide mass housing using concrete blocks for the first time in Birmingham.

The site of St Martin's flats, *c.* 1934. The site was declared a clearance area in January 1934 and altogether over 1,000 Highgate residents were displaced.

Clearing the site for the construction of St Martin's flats, *c.* 1934.

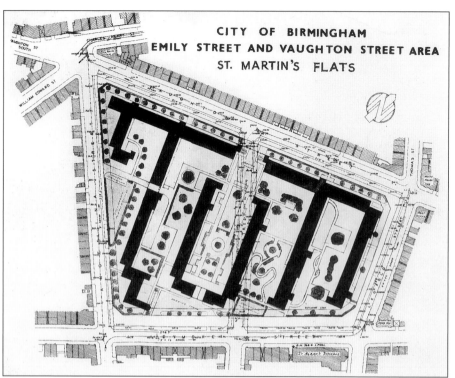

Emily and Vaughton Street Area Proposal for Development with 240 flats, four storeys high. The area of the site was 6.1 acres with 40 flats per acre; 36 were to be one bedroomed, 128 were to be two bedroomed and 76 were to be three bedroomed.

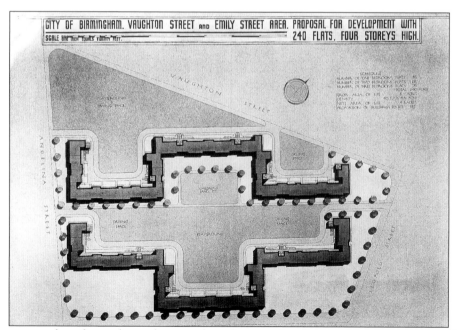

There were plans for gardens, playgrounds and even a bowling green, but the onset of the Second World War meant that the facilities offered never matched the architect's plans.

24

An architect's impression of Emily Street flats from the *Architect and Building News*, June 1937.

Construction of St Martin's flats, Emily Street, *c*. 1936. The new style flats were completed in 1939. In all, 267 flats with balconies were built. There were drying rooms on each floor and the whole scheme was originally regarded as a model development. Tenants paid rents of between 12s 6d and 15s per week for the three and four room flats.

Interior view of one of the flats shortly after construction, August 1942.

Exterior view of St Martin's flats, August 1942.

View of the flats from St Alban's church tower, 1938.

St Martin's flats shortly before demolition, looking north west from Dymoke Street, December 1979. What looked attractive on the architect's plans proved less successful in practice and in 1979 the *Evening Mail* reported that 'City Councillors had voted to tear down the rundown warren of problem flats'.

Demolition of the flats in August 1980.

The flats were finally demolished in 1981.

28

Bomb damage, Gooch Street near Sherlock Street, 30 January 1942.

Bomb damage, the River Rea at Gooch Street, 12 April 1941.

Houses in Bloomfield Road, Moseley, after a German air raid.

Air raid damage in Oxford Road, Moseley, November 1940.

Cox's Screw Factory, Charles Henry Street, Highgate, after receiving a direct hit. For a later photograph see page 47.

Oxford Road houses hit again, 16 January 1941.

Colebrook Road, 30 January 1941.

Two
Street Scenes

An early view of the Moseley Road in about 1880, showing Highgate House and Camp Hill Station.

Moseley Road junction with Brighton Road, with the Brighton Road Post Office on the corner, around the turn of the century.

Corner of Moseley Road and Park Road.

Moseley Road, nearly opposite Stratford Place, *c.* 1914.

View of Alcester Road showing the premises of Bullock and Hooper, builders. Their premises were close to where Salisbury Road was cut through to join the Alcester Road in 1896.

The novelist J.R.R. Tolkien lived here, at No. 124 Alcester Road, from 1900 to 1901. Tolkien, the author of *The Hobbit* and *The Lord of The Rings* was closely associated with Moseley. He used Sarehole Mill and the Moseley Bog in his stories and it was after the family moved from Gracewell, opposite the mill, that they moved to the Alcester Road, on the corner of Tudor Road. Tolkien described the house as 'dreadful' even though it was very convenient for the tram to his school, King Edwards in New Street. The family only stayed a short time at Alcester Road before moving to No. 86 Westfield Road.

A postcard view of Oxford Road, Moseley.

Oxford Road, showing the Baptist chapel.

Dad's Lane, Moseley, 1932. The horse and cart are from the Selly Park bakery.

Yew Tree Walk, Moor Green, *c.* 1890.

Moor Green Lane, Moseley, 1932.

Moor Green Lane, Moseley, 1932.

Underground passage, Moor Green, 1933.

Holders Lane, Moseley, 1932.

Wake Green Road, Moseley.

Mansion House, Belle Walk, Moseley, the home of the Anderton family for many years. It was the next most important house in Moseley after Moseley Hall.

Billesley Lane showing old cottages, 1912. These cottages were demolished in 1924.

Billesley Lane still presented a rural aspect into the 1920s.

'Old' Billesley Lane and Cottage.

Another view of the cottages. The photographer Sam Mason attracted some interested locals.

The new houses on Billesley Lane, 1924, captured by a photographer from the City Surveyor's Department.

Billesley Lane, 1926, with its new uncluttered look replacing the rural charm.

Another view of Billesley Lane, *c.* 1926.

The new road junction on Billesley Lane, 1926.

The Toll Gate, Moseley. The toll house was situated on the Alcester Turnpike at the top of Park Hill beside a tall fence and gate. The turnpike was originally established to bring fruit and vegetables from Worcestershire to the Birmingham market but by the nineteenth century, stage coach travellers from Moseley and Kings Heath were paying their dues at the toll gates along the route into the city.

Corner of Macdonald and Charles Henry Streets, Highgate, 1956.

Cox's Screw Factory, Charles Henry Street, 1956. See also page 31.

Numbers 17-53 Vaughton Street, Highgate, photographed by Birmingham's Public Works Department in 1956.

Corner of Gooch Street and Bissell Street, Highgate, 1960.

Charles Hofton and Sons' works in Conybere Street, 1960.

Sherlock Street, *c.* 1937.

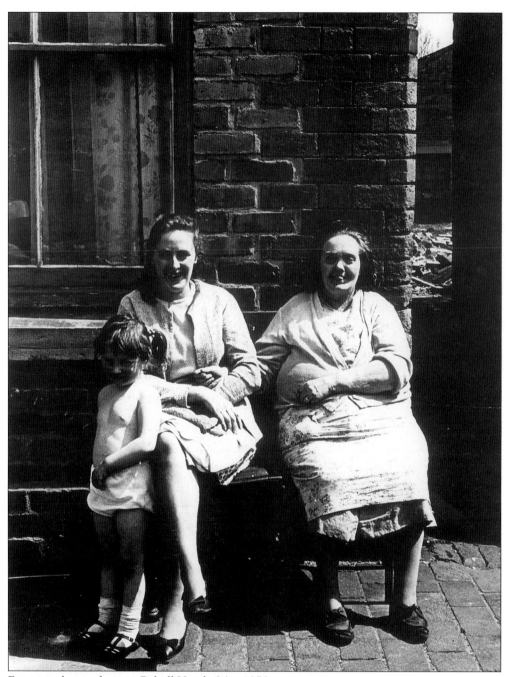

Enjoying the sunshine in Balsall Heath, May 1970.

Gooch Street shops and houses prior to redevelopment, 1966.

A street scene in Conybere Street, 1968. St Alban's church can be seen in the background.

Captured for posterity, youngsters in Balsall Heath, 1970.

Balsall Heath youngsters, 1970.

Clifton Road, Balsall Heath, with a view of the church.

Junction of Moseley Road and Belgrave Road, 1970.

Turner Street, Balsall Heath, 1968.

Balsall Heath Post Office, April 1968. In 1886 this was the home of Paul Braddon the artist. His real name was James Leslie Crees. He was born on 10 July 1864, the son of William Henry Crees, a stationers' assistant, whose family had come to England from France at the time of the French Revolution. By 1886 William Crees had settled at No. 159 Balsall Heath Road as a stationer and art dealer. It was originally intended that Leslie (as he was known) should take holy orders, but when financial circumstances forced him to abandon the idea, he began to paint. He favoured painting with water colours; his method was to make pencil sketches of buildings and scenes, with notes concerning building materials, colours and vegetation and then to paint afterwards from the sketch. Soon after the death of his father, Leslie Crees, by then better known as Paul Braddon, left Birmingham and went to live with a brother, Charles Crees in Shirley, Croydon. Leslie died aged 74 on 24 July 1938.

The Co-op on Balsall Heath Road, 8 June 1959.

Litter accumulating on Clevedon Road, Balsall Heath, 24 May 1968.

Three
Churches

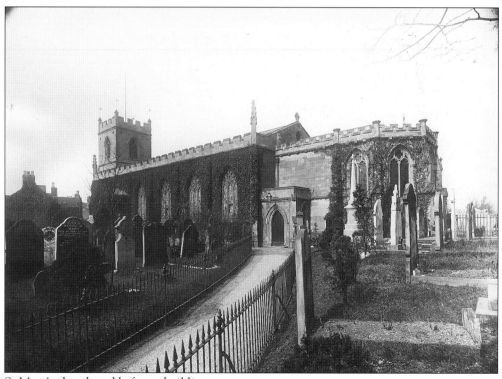

St Mary's churchyard before rebuilding.

The west end of St Agnes' church, showing the tower, 1946. There were very few houses on the far side of Billesley Lane in the 1880s, but when expansion came it was rapid. The need for a church in that area soon became felt. A temporary wooden structure was put up at the corner of Oxford Road and School Road and a competition was announced for the design of a permanent church.

St Agnes' church from the south, 1946. The competition was won by William Davis, who also designed St Paul's, Walsall Road. The church was built to his design although the tower was not completed until 1932. The temporary buildings were re-erected at St Ambrose, Pershore Road, Edgbaston. St Agnes' church stands on an island site and in 1987 was included in the Moseley Conservation Area.

Architect's drawing of Moseley Road
Baptist church.

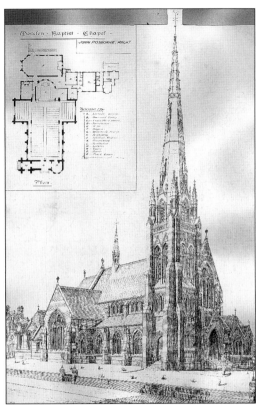

Oxford Road Baptist church.
Although the design competition
was won by William Davis,
another design put forward by
J.P. Osborne was considered to
be of very high merit. It came to
the attention of the local Baptist
congregation who were about to
build a church at the other end
of Oxford Road from St Agnes'
and it was arranged to use Mr
Osborne's designs for this
church.

The tower of St Anne's church, viewed from the road, 1946. The church was the gift of Miss Rebecca Anderton and was built on land presented by W.F. Taylor. The architect was Frederick Preedy. The church is possibly dedicated to St Anne in memory of Miss Anderton's younger sister Anne, who died less than a year before the building of the church. Construction of the church began in 1872; it was consecrated in 1874 and became a separate parish in the following year.

St Anne's church. Miss Anderton was the sole surviving member of an important Moseley family after whom Anderton Park Road is named. The church was built on the edge of what remained of the Taylor Estate. Mr W.F. Taylor, who gave the land, was from Moseley Hall. Rebecca Anderton gave several stained glass windows to the church but all were destroyed in the bomb damage of 1940.

Interior view of St Anne's church. A lasting gift of Miss Anderton's consists of the three old bells which came from St Mary's. A fourth bell was also added and hung in the tower of the new church.

Another interior view of St Anne's church in 1946, showing Second World War bomb damage. Storm damage in 1939 and 1945 and bomb damage in 1940 badly affected the church. After extensive rebuilding the roofing was completed in 1946 and the woodwork, including the floor, was restored in 1948.

St Alban's the Martyr, Conybere Street. St Alban's church, Highgate, was started in a mission establishment in 1865 by the Pollock Brothers. They survived a serious attack on their high-church rituals in 1867 and stayed for twenty-five years, according to the register on new buildings of 1913-1916. The quality of their pastoral work in the heavily populated district around the church was well received.

St Alban's church, Tower Street, 1938. The church, designed by J.I. Pearson in the thirteenth century style, was opened in 1881 and consecrated in 1899. It is still a landmark today.

St Alban's church nave. The church was well attended with a Sunday school which had 1,600 children on its register in 1887. On one occasion a summer excursion took place with 1,189 children, 210 teachers and a brass band marching from Leopold Street to Camp Hill Station to board the excursion trains.

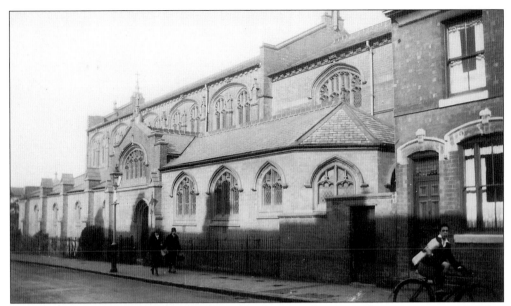

St Barnabas church, Balsall Heath. The church opened as a tin hut mission in 1890 but energetic fund raising enabled the new building to be opened in 1904. An advertisement stated that the parish of Balsall Heath, with a population of 35,000, requires £2,000 to complete and finish the building exclusive of the tower.

Interior of St Barnabas church, Balsall Heath. Unfortunately the church was partly destroyed during the Second World War.

St Paul's church, Balsall Heath, 1873. Some time around 1850 a young clergyman, the Revd Benison, visited Balsall Heath to look for a house for his relatives. He found the area to his liking with its open fields which lay behind the railway towards Ladypool Lane and the River Rea, which lay in the other direction and was still a sparkling stream lined with berry bushes. The only item the area seemed to lack was a church.

St Paul's church, Balsall Heath. In May 1850 seven gentlemen met in Edward Townsend Cox's house, Balsall Heath, to discuss ways and means of building a church. A public meeting followed in The Waggon and Horses on Moseley Road and in 1852 work finally stared on the building of the church. It was consecrated the following year in a blaze of publicity. The church had seating for 1,111 people of which 500 seats were allocated to the congregation by name.

Congregational church, Balsall Heath, 1873. Particularly impressive are the twin spires of the church, which opened in 1862, with seating for a thousand people.

St Mary's church, Moseley, 1812. In February 1405 Pope Innocent VII issued a licence to the Bishop of Worcester for a Chapel of Saint Mary in Moseley, because the parish church of Kings Norton was considered too far distant for the needs of local people. In 1494 the wife of Henry VII gave some waste land in Moseley for the building of a chapel. This was the site of the present church. Although we do not know when the church was built, we do know that that the steeple was added in 1513.

St Mary's church. The chapel fell into disrepair in the late eighteenth century and in 1778 the roof fell in so a public subscription was raised to rebuild the church between 1780 and 1782. In 1823 the church was enlarged, the architect being Thomas Rickman and in 1853, Moseley was created into a parish separate from Kings Norton. Further improvements took place in 1857 when a public clock was installed in the tower and in 1866, when gas lighting was installed in the church.

St Mary's church, 15 March 1909. The church was again extended in 1870, 1909 and 1910. A number of windows by well known twentieth century makers, including C.E. Kemp and Co. of London and Birmingham's firm of John Hardman and Co., can be seen in the church.

The Wesleyan chapel, Moseley Road, before 1885.

Highgate Baptist church, Moseley Road, 1935.

Four

Transport

Steam tram, 1906.

Postcard view of the horse coaches plying for trade at Moseley Village.

Climbing aboard a steam tram in 1902. A regular horse drawn bus service from Moseley to Birmingham commenced in 1859.

A steam tram in 1867, the same year that Moseley Station was opened, to be replaced in turn by electrically-powered trams in 1906.

Steam tram on the Moseley Road in Balsall Heath in the winter of 1906.

A British Red Cross van encountering difficulties in the snow on the way to Moor Green Hospital.

Horse buses plied from Moseley Village to central Birmingham ten times a day from about 1860 until competition from trams made the service obsolete.

The model railway in the gardens of Pitmaston, the home of St John and Lady Holder. It was regarded as one of the sights of Birmingham.

Pitmaston Terminus.

Moseley Station from a photograph by Thomas Lewis reproduced in *Birmingham Faces and Places*. The accompanying text states 'There is no prettier station or one more picturesque situated than that which was opened at Moseley about seventeen years ago... when it was opened only a few passenger trains ran between Moseley and Birmingham but now (1890) owing to the great and rapid growth of population, about thirty trains run to and from these stations every day'.

Moseley Station, 1900.

Moseley Station showing the old wooden bridge which gave its name to Woodbridge Road and was replaced by a brick structure.

The old bridge on the Brighton Road, Balsall Heath, in 1923. The view was taken by Birmingham City's Surveyor's Department showing the need to widen the road.

Construction of the new bridge, September 1924.

Balsall Heath Station, Brighton Road, March 1924.

Five
Moseley Village

Moseley Village, 1873.

When this photograph was reproduced in *Birmingham Faces and Places* in 1889 it came with the following description, 'We present our readers with a view of Moseley Village as it looked before the tramways had laid their lines of steel round it, and before the green had been railed round with iron railings and made 'genteel', with a modern lamp of typical nineteenth century construction at each corner of its triangle. The Old Bulls Head has made way for a modern brick structure and the cottages have been taken down to make room for the erection of shops of the ultra-modern type. The old church still watches over the village and the same old tower remains, which for hundreds of years has been a landmark in the district. The time to observe the present popularity of Moseley is on a fine Sunday afternoon when tramcar and bus vie with each other in depositing their loads of people here, either to attend afternoon service at the church, or to make excursions after fresh air in the country lanes and in the fields.'

Early view of Moseley Village by Thomas Lewis.

Early view of Moseley Village by Thomas Lewis.

Moseley Village Green 'as it is proposed' in 1893.

After the redevelopment, 1895.

Traffic was slightly different ninety years ago!

Alcester Road at the village showing the junction with Salisbury Road, which was cut in the 1890s through the Moseley Hall Estate and turned the village into a cross roads. Salisbury Road was named after the then Prime Minister, Lord Salisbury.

St Mary's, leading down to the village, photographed in 1946.

A post war view of the village.

Fighting Cocks coach, mid 1890s. There has been a Fighting Cocks in the row of buildings leading to the village since the late eighteenth century. There were at least two major rebuildings in the 1860s, when the inn was turned into a large hotel with gardens and a bowling green and in 1899, when the present terracotta pub was built.

A trade card for the Fighting Cocks. The name itself is a reminder that cock fighting once took place on the Green.

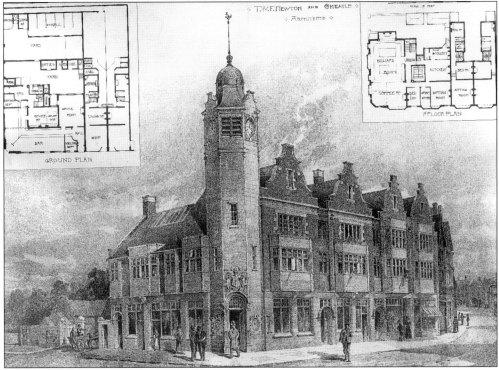

Illustration of the Fighting Cocks from the *Building News*, 8 December 1899. The Holte Brewery took over the pub in 1899, replaced the old hotel with shops and moved the pub to its present corner site. The architects for the new building were Newton and Cheatle, a prestigious firm specialising in city centre arcades and offices. Their stylish interior fittings have earned the Fighting Cocks a Grade II listed status. The barometer and wind directional dial in the wall at the foot of the pub were placed there because of the meteorological interests of a Holte Brewery director.

The Fighting Cocks, 1974. The tower had a weather cock on top mounted on a spike and geared to the compass at the bottom.

Six

Moseley Hall, Highbury and Spring Hill College

Relaxing on the lawns at Highbury Hall, home of the Chamberlains.

Moseley Hall, the residence of Lady Carhampton from an engraving by William Ellis, published in 1792. The first Moseley Hall stood somewhere to the north of St Mary's church. Owned by the Grevis family, they later owned a large timber framed building which probably stood near to the present entrance to Moseley Park. The last remnants were demolished around 1942.

Moseley Hall from an engraving, 1831. The grounds of Moseley Hall at one time extended along the west side of Alcester Road from Edgbaston Lane to the Queensbridge roundabout. There were three entrances to the grounds. The Grevis family fell upon hard times in the eighteenth century and Moseley Hall was sold to John Taylor, of Bordesley Park, a wealthy button manufacturer.

Moseley Hall and Park. Taylor never lived at the Hall. He died in 1775 and was succeeded by his son, also named John. He built a mansion of brick and stone in Moseley Park, at a cost of £6,000; this stood near the site of the present Moseley Hall. In July, during the Priestley Riots, Moseley Hall was attacked and set on fire. Taylor, a dissenter, was not in Birmingham at the time, but he did claim nearly £4,000 damages. He was awarded about two thirds of that amount.

Moseley Hall, the proposed sanatorium for women and children. The Hall was rebuilt between 1792 and 1796, the architect being John Standbridge of Warwick. The Taylors sold the estate in several sections, mostly towards the end of the nineteenth century. The Hall was bought by Richard Cadbury, the chocolate manufacturer, who lived there from 1884 to 1891.

View of the park from behind the sanatorium, taken from a postcard sent in 1905. Richard Cadbury gave Moseley Hall to Birmingham City Council to become a children's convalescent home.

View of the Hall from the drive. The Hall is now a hospital and run by the Local Health Authority.

The Park, showing the sunk fence, in 1908.

A closer view of the sunk fence at
Moseley Hall, 1908.

Richard Cadbury, who was born on 6 November 1768. In 1794 Richard Tapper Cadbury left a well established family wool-combing business in Devon for the attractions of the developing industrial Midlands. He opened a silk and drapery shop in Bull Street, which at the time was the principal business throughfare in a town which was still predominantly rural in its outlook. The Birmingham magazine *Edgbastonia* wrote, ' To within a few weeks of the close of his life, his figure was a familiar one in our streets. He adhered to the formal simplicity of 'cut' characteristic of the attire of the members of the Society of Friends, but was always careful and even smartly, dressed. Few people met him without raising the hat in token of respect. He was greatly esteemed by his co-religionists, over whom his influence was so great that, amongst them, he was unusually spoken of as 'King Richard'. He died in 1860 at the age of 92.'

'Little Patients' in the grounds.

Moseley Park.

Moseley Park entrance.

Postcard view of Highbury Hall and Joseph Chamberlain, Birmingham's best known politician. He commenced the building of Highbury Hall at Moor Green in 1878 and it was his home from 1880 to 1914. He named it Highbury after the London suburb where he spent his childhood.

Highbury from the imposing drive. The house was designed by another Chamberlain, the architect John Henry Chamberlain (not a relative) and is an outstanding example of a prosperous late Victorian family residence.

Highbury showing the conservatory. With a staff of eighteen gardeners Chamberlain and his guests could enjoy the splendours of the house and its grounds.

The drawing room in the 1890s. It was used by the Chamberlains for receiving visitors in the afternoon and for entertaining guests after dinner.

The main hall in the 1890s. It occupies the whole central area of the house and could be used for receptions or private functions.

The library in about 1900. The carved bookcases were brought from Chamberlain's previous home in Edgbaston and re-fitted at Highbury. The window was designed by John Hardman and Company.

The conservatory. Chamberlain built up a magnificent orchid collection here and in the thirteen glasshouses at Highbury.

The extensive grounds showing the small pool. The pool was formed from an existing stream on the estate.

A landscape gardener, Edward Milner, was responsible for the design of the extensive grounds.

Rehabilitation. After Chamberlain's death in 1914 the house was no longer used by the family. During the First World War it was used as an annexe to the First Southern General Hospital and then as a home for disabled ex-servicemen.

The tailor's shop, 1915.

A group of patients and nurses.

Taking advantage of the facilities.

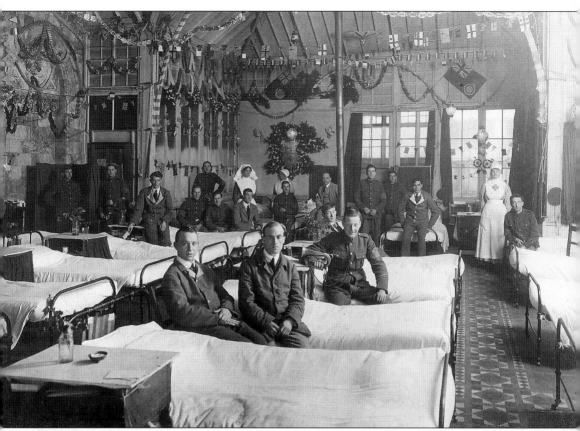

Ward 5a.

Spring Hill College, 1868. Spring Hill College was so called because it had been originally founded in a road of that name near Hockley. It came into being through a bequest in the will of Charles Glover, who died in 1821, to provide a college and equipment for the training of Congregational ministers.

A side view taken by Thomas Lewis for the Warwickshire Photographic Survey, 1868. By the 1850s the building had become inadequate for its purpose and a new site on Wake Green Road was purchased. Work started on the much larger building in 1854 and was completed in 1857. The college buildings were later adapted to use as a school. An extract from the diary of a boy in Class 2X, 11 September 1923, reads, 'I get out of bed - it is 9.15 a.m. I make my way towards Moseley Secondary School and reach same at 9.35 a.m. I am instantly filled with awe at the site of the dull red bricked pile of stones - my friend is struck also and talks in a strange, whispering unreasonable voice'.

The entrance while it was still a college. The architect was Joseph James and the building is a good example of the decorated style of Gothic Revival. The College moved to Oxford under the name of Mansfield College some thirty years later. It is not clear what the building was used for between the years of 1886 to 1892, but in the latter year it was bought by a Mr Ross who renamed it the Pine Dell Hydropathic Establishment; springs under the building provided natural spa water. The boarding fees were five shillings per day, or seven shillings if the full hydropathic treatment was taken.

The Moseley Botanical Gardens, *c.* 1893. At the same time as the Pine Dell Hydropathic Establishment was started, the Moseley Botanical Gardens were opened in the corner of the grounds adjacent to Wake Green Road and College Road. These ventures lasted for less than a decade.

The cloister-like corridors photographed by Thomas Lewis. In 1923 the building was acquired by Birmingham Education Committee and the Secondary School was opened on 11 September. It was renamed Moseley Grammar School in 1939 and being of special architectural and historical interest, became a listed building in 1972.

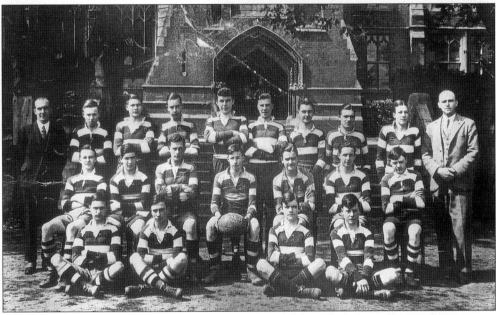

Moseley School Rugby Team, 1928, outside the school. The fixture for the 1928/1929 season included both state and grammar schools. Matches were played against Burton, Camp Hill, Sutton and Halesowen Grammar Schools and Yardley, Central and George Dixon State Schools, but poor weather meant that, as the school magazine reported, 'Many of our football half days have been devoted to skating parades'.

The college buildings were used as a training centre for the 3rd Birmingham City Battalion during the Great War.

The college was subsequently used as a rehabilitation centre for ex-servicemen.

Seven
Arts and Leisure

The reading room, Balsall Heath Library, 1910.

Tram passing along the Moseley Road outside the Balsall Heath Library and Swimming Baths. In 1891 Balsall Heath gave up its independence and joined Birmingham; in return it was promised a library and baths. These flamboyant buildings in glazed brick and terracotta were the fulfilment of that promise.

Balsall Heath branch library shortly after its opening in 1896.

The library, nearly one hundred years later and still valued by the local community. The prominent coat of arms of Birmingham were a constant reminder to passing residents of Moseley and Kings Heath of the advantages of joining Birmingham. Moseley gave up its independence in 1911.

The library interior, 1910. All the books were on closed access and the reading tables discouraged any mixing of the sexes.

The exterior of the Balsall Heath Swimming Baths soon after it opened. The official opening by the Lord Mayor took place on 30 October 1907, eleven years after the library, because of difficulties arising from securing an adequate water supply.

Literally the same view in 1992. This photograph is copyright of the Birmingham Picture Library, a valuable source of contemporary photographs of Birmingham.

The ticket office where bathers could buy either first or second class tickets.

Interior of the first class swimming baths.

Private bath departments for men.

The interior of the boiler house.

One of the two steam boilers of the Lancashire type which supplied the steam for the various departments of the baths and which heated the water in the two swimming baths.

The private bath departments for women.

Interior of the second class swimming baths.

Opposite: The Alhambra entrance. Behind its conventional facade the Alhambra offered a new and exciting concept in cinema design. The interior was pure Moorish based on the Alhambra Palace in Granada, Spain, so that picture-goers stepped off the Moseley Road straight into a Moorish courtyard.

112

The Alhambra Cinema. The Alhambra was the largest and best known of several competing picture houses on the Moseley Road between Highgate and Moseley Village. The cinema was built on the site of the eighteenth century Moseley Theatre. It opened on Boxing Day 1928 with a screening of *The Pimpernel* staring Mattherson Lang.

The auditorium at the Alhambra. The cinema could seat over 1,200 in its circle and stalls. The crowning jewel of the splendid auditorium was the central ceiling light, a six foot wide glass bowl representing the sun, set in a blue mediterranean sky.

The Alhambra: ABC monitors. The Alhambra, along with other picture houses in the same chain, was taken over by the ABC Group and became the Moseley ABC. The doorman, monitors and usherettes all contributed to the corporate theme. However, changing public tastes led to the closing of many suburban cinemas including the Alhambra which closed on 31 August 1968, after a final screening of *The Fall of the Roman Empire*. It was then used as an Asian cinema for several years before being pulled down.

The Triangle Cinema. The picture house on the corner of Gooch Street and Conybere Street was originally opened in 1915 as Pringles Picture Palace. The building itself was a converted chapel.

Side view of the Triangle in Gooch Street, taken in 1955. The picture house was rebuilt in 1923 and in recognition of its site became the Triangle. In later years it became Birmingham's first Asian cinema and was subsequently demolished.

Moseley Picture House. This was one of the earliest cinemas in Birmingham. Sited on the Moseley Road, it opened on 12 May 1913 and it operated as a cinema until 1974 when it was demolished to make way for the widening of the Moseley Road. Like most other cinemas in the area it had shown Asian films in its last years.

Balsall Heath Picture House. Situated on the Balsall Heath Road near Longmore Street, the cinema was originally going to have been called the Balsall Heath Picturedome. It opened in 1913 and could seat 650. In the 1940s its name changed to the Luxor Cinema; it then became an Asian cinema and finally closed in 1983.

The New Imperial Picture House, Moseley Road, 1946. Another cinema on the Moseley Road, the Imperial was opposite the junction with Edward Road. It opened on Monday 26 January 1914 and closed in 1983. An advertisement in 1916 promised ' You are always sure of a high class and pleasing programme at the little Imperial'. It is remembered as a select and dignified picture house showing better films and charging higher prices.

Friends Meeting House on the Moseley Road. The building has been the meeting place of numerous local educational and cultural groups for many years.

Among some of the groups who used the Meeting House for many years were the Adult School Union, the Dolobran Athletic Club and the Men's Early Morning School.

Moseley and Balsall Heath Institute. The origins of the Institute were the Mechanics Institutes with their mission of self-improvement for Victorian artisans. The Institute was built in 1893 on land on the Moseley Road donated by two of its lady members. It was opposite their own house, the White House, on the corner of Edgbaston Road.

A postcard view of the Institute, often spoken of as the Town Hall of Moseley.

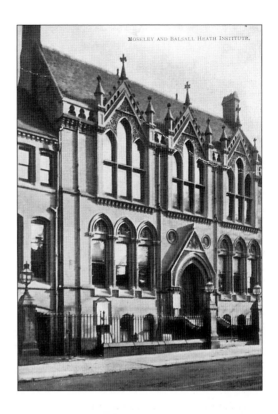

The Tennyson room which was used for whist drives and dancing.

The Institute's committee of 1926-1927.

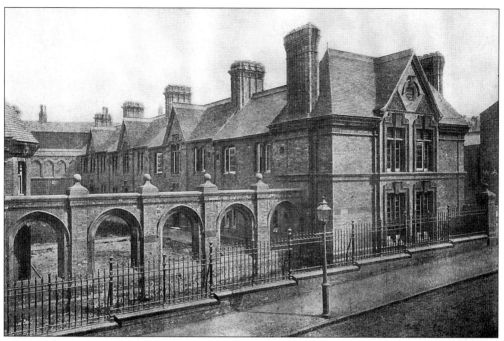

Lenches Trust Almshouses, Conybere Street, Highgate.

The Almshouses.

Moseley Quoit and Bowling Club, 1875. Membership was by invitation only, with a black ball system of one black ball in five enough to exclude membership. The club was, of course, for gentlemen only. Membership cost three guineas with an annual subscription of one guinea. Rule ten unequivocally stated, 'no betting allowed on any game'.

Opposite: Moseley golf clubhouse, c. 1914. The club was formed in 1892 with just twelve founder members. A nine hole course was established on land in Billesley Lane on the borders of Kings Heath and Moseley. Rent of the ground was £10 a year and upkeep of the course cost £15. In 1908 more land was added and another nine holes were built. The course was extensively remodelled and extended again just prior to the First World War.

The Midland Counties Rugby Team who played Yorkshire at the Reddings, Moseley, on 10 February 1892; Yorkshire won by one goal and two tries to nil. The Reddings, in Reddings Road, has been the home of Moseley Rugby Football Club, Birmingham's premier side, since 1880. The club had been formed seven years before as Havelock Football Club but within a year had adopted both the name Moseley and the red and black colours which have continued ever since.

The clubhouse interior.

Highgate Park and Rowton House, 1932.

124

Rowton House. One of the most prominent landmarks in the area, Rowton House or the Chamberlain Hotel as it is now, still evokes the question 'what is it?' The general consensus is that it must have been the workhouse. In fact the grand, but slightly forbidding building on the edge of Highgate Park, has always been a hotel. It was built in 1903 and named Rowton House after Lord Rowton who founded a chain of ' poor man's hotels'. When it opened it could sleep 800 men a night, each paying the sixpence necessary for a sparse but clean bedroom. As a contemporary report concluded, 'Its own healthy tone and surroundings react upon the lodgers, keep up their self respect, safeguard them against evil assignations and induce them to rise!'

The Chamberlain Hotel. In 1958 it was renamed the Highgate Hotel and was at one time threatened with closure. However in the 1990s it was enterprisingly and attractively converted into a three star hotel and again renamed the Chamberlain Hotel. It is much in demand for seminars and training events.

Highgate Park tennis and bowls pavilion. The site of Highgate Park was the first open space bought by Birmingham. In more rural days it had been used to graze sheep and it had afforded a fine view of the town, indeed some of the earliest views of Birmingham were taken from here. It was in May 1875 that Birmingham Corporation paid £8,000 for Highgate Fields and within a year the mayor, Joseph Chamberlain, opened the four acre park, which was initially going to be named Camp Hill Park but this was felt to sound too much like the nearby Cannon Hill Park.

Statue of Edward VII. This statue was re-erected in Highgate Park in February 1951, having been in Victoria Square in the city centre. It had been unveiled in 1913 and shows the King in the uniform of a Field Marshal wearing the Coronation Robe. The sculptor was Albert Toft. The cost of £2,700 was paid for by public subscription as part of a memorial to the King.

Vandalism in the park. Park policeman R. David surveys the damage in December 1960.

Balsall Heath Park, 1963.

Balsall Heath Park, 1963. The park opened shortly after Balsall Heath joined the City and along with the baths and library was another indication of Birmingham's civic responsibility. The four acre park was created on the site of the old, drained Lady Pool, after which the road was named.

Rural charm of the allotments at Moor Green captured for the Warwickshire Photographic Survey in 1933.